Quick & Easy Solutions:
How to Increase
Mobile Notary
Business for More
Success & Profit
with 37 Professional Tips

by DERRICK SPRUILL

Book edited by Lee Lee Trotter

Cover design, interior photos, and illustrations by Montes
Travis

ISBN: 979-8-218-19752-0

DEDICATION

I dedicate this book to my family. For all the support and encouragement during the countless hours, I invested over the years into this passion for building a business to serve others. I want to especially thank my parents, Blanche, and Xavier Spruill, for making me into the son I am today. Thank you.

CONTENTS

ACKNOWLEDGMENTS

I want to acknowledge many people who helped me become who I am today. Right now, I am right where I'm supposed to be because of all the people I have encountered over the years. Thanks to my first family, my last family, my brothers, my sisters, my parents, my extended family, my current family, past friends, my colleagues at all my places of work over the years, the relationships I have made along the way, including those from attending college, bible studies, and anyone else who knows me. I acknowledge you.

Chapter 1

What is

MOBILE NOTARY?

Finally, I finished my last course at Walden University and graduated. Now, I had to decide what to do after receiving my MBA in Human Resources. I, unfortunately, did not have a new endeavor to go with my degree. Although my role in leadership at my current job was satisfying, I knew I wanted to contribute more. All the knowledge and skill we may have is a gift we can give to help others. These abilities can be used inside or outside of the workplace. As I often do, I remember thoughts I had about ten years ago about being a Notary Public, one that conducted traveling services (mobile). Why? Well, I'll tell you more about that a little later.

So, what is a traveling mobile notary? So, let's use the term mobile notary going forward. A mobile notary, put, is an official witness who travels to someone to sign documents to verify that the person or persons signing the documents are who they say they are. The mobile notary may charge up to the maximum fee set by state law for notarization services. In some states, a mobile notary may also charge a separate travel fee for traveling to the customer's location. I have been a mobile notary since 2018, serving Loudon County, Fairfax County, and Prince William County in Virginia, and I enjoy serving the public.

I first thought I could fill my time studying this craft and become a master at it and be my very own boss. I could travel to places I never traveled before and meet people I never knew. This could be fulfilling. I started researching and reading everything I could about the mobile notary work and guidelines governing Virginia.

I discovered that mobile notaries are typically used for real estate or mortgage transactions. Still, they can also be used for general notary work and notarizing other types of documents, such as wills, power of attorney, sale of property, apostille services, i9 documentation, process serving, document delivery, document retrieval from the courthouse, wedding officiant, promissory note, settlement agreements, consent forms, residential lease agreement, adoption papers, fingerprinting service, skip tracing, medical authorization for minors, bank transfer service, authentication of documents, advanced health directives, and others.

Wow, that's a lot to study, but I've been reading a lot over the years, and what's a little more studying is going to hurt. I'm unable to sleep all night already. I also had to remember that a notary is a commissioned public official and servant of the state. A notary that performs these notary tasks must be trustworthy with the highest level of integrity regarding all the legal bidding documents they encounter.

That was not a problem, I encounter many human resource issues at work and comb through mountains of sensitive work documents every day, so I said I could do this, and having the title commissioned public official sounds professional.

Illustration by Montes Travis

To become a mobile notary, I must first be a notary public. I applied to my state's Secretary of State to become a notary public. I never needed to visit that website, so this was a first. Once I become a notary public, I could start offering mobile notary services.

Mobile notaries are also known as:

On-site notaries
Traveling notaries
A notary public who comes to you
A notary public who travels to you
A notary public who will come to your home or office.

There are many benefits for people to use a mobile notary. The first is convenience. The public can have the notary travel to them, so they do not have to go to a notary's office, postage delivery store location, or banking institution. Second, it saves time. Mobile notaries typically charge a travel fee, but often a person's time is more valuable than this travel fee. Third, it is more private. The customer can have the notary come to their home instead of the customer going to an office or a public storefront. They do not have to worry about signing documents in the presence of others, like a husband and wife needing a divorce settlement agreement.

Here is a list of services that mobile notaries can provide:

Notarize signatures on documents.
Witness the signing of documents.
Ensure that the singer is who they say they are.
Verify the authenticity of documents.
Ensure that the signer is signing the document voluntarily.
Provide a notary seal on documents.

Mobile notaries must be licensed and insured, and we must follow all the same rules and regulations as traditional notaries. We also must take an oath of office, which means we are legally bound to uphold the law. In addition, mobile notaries are often bonded, meaning we have insurance that will cover any damage we may cause during our work.

Then the lightbulb went off. Make it official and build a business and incorporate from the ground up. Come up with the name and become a true professional. So, I started thinking, what should I do first? Name of business? After looking up mobile notaries near me on the Internet, I settled on the name Mobile Notary by Derrick Spruill. Plain, nothing fancy, but then I started working on the logo, and wow, it looked just right. That was the artistic skill I had been putting to work. The logo looked like a business that's been around for years with the simple notary stamp seal and lettering that helps customers understand my services. A year later, we had the logo redesigned as a courtesy of a good friend.

Then I thought, why would a customer reach out to

me, and what would make me stand out from all the other notaries? I know how I use the internet to search for services I need, so that is how others would look for me through the World Wide Web. It is always essential for customers to do their research before hiring any professional, and mobile notaries are no exception. They can check with the state's notary public office to make sure that the mobile notary they are considering is licensed and insured. They may also read online reviews to understand other people's experiences with the notary.

So, my thinking continued, I need to build a level of trust for a customer to trust that I will not make a mistake with their documents, and they can verify whom I say I am. Funny, affirming the notary, but true. I need to prove who I am first.

By listing these concerns in a thought bubble and writing solutions out on a whiteboard, how could I be hired as a reputable and trustworthy mobile notary was the question I was trying to answer.

Illustration and photo by Montes Travis

I need to ask for references from friends and family.
I need to check the notary's website or online reviews.
I need to make sure the notary is licensed and insured.
I need to ask the notary about their experience and qualifications.
I must research the notary's name online, using the internet and searching social sites on the World Wide Web.
I need to look for pictures of the notary.

Later in this book, I will share 37 Professional Tips answering these questions that help put the public at ease when hiring me to conduct a notarization for them.

TIME TO TAKE NOTES
Exercise 1.

What will differentiate you as a mobile notary in your area?

What will be your service hours and the territory you will serve?

Why would someone seek you out for mobile notary services?

Illustration and photo by Montes Travis

Chapter 2

Why Become a

MOBILE NOTARY?

As I promised to let you know, I remembered when the time was right that I needed to become a mobile notary because of an incident that occurred in Norfolk, Virginia, about ten years earlier. I was at the hospital with my wife, and we needed a notary for my ailing mother-in-law on a Saturday morning. We could not find any notary available to help us in our great time of need. It was the most stressful 48 hours of our lives. God be the glory; my mother-in-law still lives today during this writing. I believe no one should have gone through the stress and anxiety of not being able to acquire a service they may need or feel they may need in moments of uncertainty. I have been serving so many people over the last few years as a notary has been honored to travel to nursing homes, rehabilitation centers, hospitals, luxury retirement facilities deep in the mountains, and out into the open countryside to visit people who could not travel and serve those with limited access to special abilities. I think about how many of us are so privileged to go about our day taking instant access and mobility for granted. I feel so humbled thinking about the five senses I possess and my ability to go anywhere I please and take the opportunity to do anything I want when I want to do it. Some do not have that same access. So, when I can help others in their time of need, I try my best to help others by bending over backward and going that extra mile whenever I can.

I have a regular work schedule outside of being a notary, and there are times late at night when somebody needs service after my long workday, but I still want to help.

Sometimes my customers call me at 4:00 AM before work, and I still want to help. There are times after a long day of running errands when everything has gone wrong, and my mind is tired, and I still would want to help. I help because I may need help when I least expect it. I have seen it many times over the last few years, and I would want somebody to extend their hand to me when I need that having a human mind sense. Call it paying it forward or serving people.

Illustration by Montes Travis

I traveled to the airport just before a father was about to take his daughter overseas as he had forgotten to get a signed document with consent and permission from his wife. I have had to travel to a business meeting to notarize a record for the president of a company at the very last minute. I was so glad I was able to help. I had a customer who had to make a declaration before traveling to a different country after an earthquake in their home country. I was so glad I was able to help. I notarized many other documents over the years, like

14

when a company hires candidates in a different state needing the I9 employment documentation verified. At other times, family members needed a document witnessed and notarized to ensure all parties were bound by their agreements. Couples on the verge of divorce needed privacy in their homes out of the public's eye, and I was glad to help. I do enjoy serving the public. I take so much pride in helping so many people in their private lives, assisting in these moments in this life journey. I hope you find your reason for serving the public, and I hope it makes you happy to want to be a notary or a mobile notary.

TIME TO TAKE NOTES
Exercise 2.

What is your purpose?

What drives you?

What do you wish to accomplish?

16

Chapter 3

Starting the business

Initially, I pondered what kind of business structure I should establish. Having just completed my degree, I knew much research was needed. I investigated all the different types of business structures and answered that age-old question. Which one is right for me? The decision was made to go with a corporate network. Some may decide to use an LLC, and some may choose to be sole proprietors. *I cannot advise you on which one to choose, but once you select it, you can proceed to the next step. I am not an attorney, and I do not have a law degree, so none of the information is meant to be considered legal advice.*

There are great benefits between these structures, so please conduct your due diligence in researching the difference and choose wisely in the beginning because it may cost you time and money later to make these changes. Next, I decided on a name for my business and a logo to go with it. You can go all out by determining which specific colors mean, which shapes may be attractive, or even the type of words that might convey a message that you want to impact your customer base. We decided to go with Mobile Notary by Derrick Spruill. Simple, straightforward. It works, putting the pressure on myself to live up to integrity in being the best. Who wants to associate their name with subpar? The next step was to register the business with the state. Our company took birth on October 8th, which was Columbus Day. The official birthday of our business, wow! It took less than a day to become official. On October 9th, we went to the bank with our documents to open a business checking and savings account with the official business name. That was an exciting day. Then the next step was enhancing our website from using our name to a legal business name. The excitement ensued. The following are the steps to getting through the beginning steps for us.

Here are a few steps we used in starting our business:

1. Write a business plan. A business plan is a roadmap for your business that will help you stay on track. It should include information about your business model, the target market or counties you will serve, the marketing strategy for reaching those customers, financial projections, and how much you expect to make and how much it will cost you in time.

2. Choose a business structure. There are several different business structures to choose from. The structures are sole proprietorship, partnership, corporations, S corporations, and limited liability. Each with its advantages and disadvantages. You should select the proper structure for your business based on liability, taxes, and ownership.

3. Get the necessary permits and licenses from the county or state. You can find information about the permits and licenses you need on your state's website or from the Small Business Administration.

4. Register your business name. You must register your business name with the state if you are not doing business as a sole proprietorship. You can register your business name on your state's corporation commission website. Once you get your employer identification number (when not using your social security number), or if you are incorporating, you may need to establish by-laws, good standing with the state, and more.

Review your state's guidelines for more information and do your research.

5. Open a business bank account. Opening a bank account is essential to separate your personal and business finances. This will make it easier to track your business expenses and income.

6. Get errors and omission insurance. There are several types of professional insurance you may need for your business. You should talk to an insurance agent to determine what kind of insurance you need. We obtained insurance in our first years with a national association before obtaining E&O insurance with our auto and homeowners insurance company.

7. Market your business. Once you have everything else, it's time to start marketing your business. There are several ways to market your business: online marketing, print advertising, public relations, passing out business cards, yard signs, car door magnets, t-shirts, and more.

8. Set the pricing structure for your business. Once your business is running, you must know what you will charge for your different services. We set our prices from the very beginning. I would ask people occasionally, "What is your number? I mean, what are you worth? What do you need to manage your finances versus your private time?" Once we initially set our prices, we did not change our prices. We are not the highest, and we are not the lowest. We found a sweet spot where we feel comfortable traveling to see a

customer after working a long grueling day at our full-time job.

9. Decide how customers will contact you. We used an 800 number with a virtual phone service that lets us know when a notary customer calls for service. There are other third-party number forwarding services you can acquire. Some may use other internet service provider numbers or their private number. Just remember, sometimes what goes on the internet stays on the internet for a long time or forever.

10. How to accept payments. There are several options: cash, check, credit, and debit cards. One day, I was asked by upper leadership at my full-time job, "Why are we making these customers wait to pay us?" Lightbulb, this pain point should not exist. Since then, I made it a point to make it as easy as possible for customers to give us their money. We have enjoyed such great benefits from using Square over the years. Easy to use by tap, dip, or swipe. Recently, we can now use the tap feature with the RF or RFID or radio frequency contactless credit card software without the hardware directly on our phone. We have had customers who wanted to pay by other forms of payment. So, over the years, as we come across those customers, we set up professional services to take those payment options.

Starting a business is a lot of work but can also be rewarding. If you are willing to put in the time and effort, you can be successful in business.

Here are the most common business structures:

Sole proprietorship: A sole proprietorship is a business owned and operated by one person. The owner is personally liable for all debts and obligations of the company.

Partnership: A partnership is a business owned by two or more people. The partners are jointly liable for all debts and obligations of the company.

Limited liability company (LLC): An LLC is a hybrid business structure that combines a corporation's limited liability with a partnership's tax benefits. The owners of an LLC are called members, and they are not personally liable for the debts and obligations of the business.

Corporation: A corporation is a business that its shareholders own. The shareholders are not personally liable for the debts and obligations of the corporation.

S corporation: An S corporation is a corporation that has elected to be taxed as a partnership. The shareholders of an S-corporation are not personally liable for the debts and obligations of the corporation.

BRAINSTORM BUSINESS NAMES & LOGOS.
Exercise 3.

Illustration and photo by Montes Travis

Chapter 4

What prices to charge?

Time for more research to be conducted. I needed to find out how much people are willing to pay for a mobile notary to travel to homes, businesses, retirement centers, hospitals, and anywhere else. I started looking online to see what the prices were listed. I looked from California to Delaware using several major search engines on the Internet with location tracking off and found very few prices listed for viewing by mobile notaries. The few prices I did find for a mobile notary were too complex, involved cost per mile plus time, and so forth. I found other prices that were too low. I did find one company listed from coast to coast that was high for the regular consumer. They are more for wealthier consumers who demand quick turnaround or immediate services. Could I provide that type of service? I would not be able to provide such a service. I conducted more analysis. What is my time worth? If I had a customer to call me at 6 p.m. for an 8 p.m. appointment, how long would it take me to get dressed, drive to the client, complete the notary assignment, drive back home, and get undressed? I would still need to return to where I was before the client called. We took all that into account when setting the pricing. Once we decided on the pricing, we published it. We accounted for credit card processing fees, the cost of travel, and the cost of toll roads. We traveled within a 30-mile radius of the local airport; the standard price was just right.

Later we configured all the other prices over time and added them to our website and an online data collection form for clients to book a notary online. Using an online data collection form removes all doubt about service pricing. When a customer enters their name and address, picks the date and time, selects the service, and enters their credit card information, all doubt is removed about the price. So, after having many customers use this online form to book services, we found our ideal customer satisfied with the pricing structure. We added administration pricing for printing documents. We added mailing services with prices that cover the cost of postal shipping. We started offering additional witnesses for an additional charge. We decided on a standard fee for loan signings and apostille services. We wanted customers to know the prices for our services before we met. So, we decided to list our prices for the public to see. A standard price where everyone was charged the same fee for the same service regardless of our starting location. This strategy has proven to be quite successful.

You will have to decide on the prices you are comfortable with. What is your value? What are clients willing to pay you? What will they get for the cost of your services? And do you feel good about the prices you have set? We are in it for the long term. The growth in our customer count has increased by 50% each year, and our revenue has increased by the same amount.

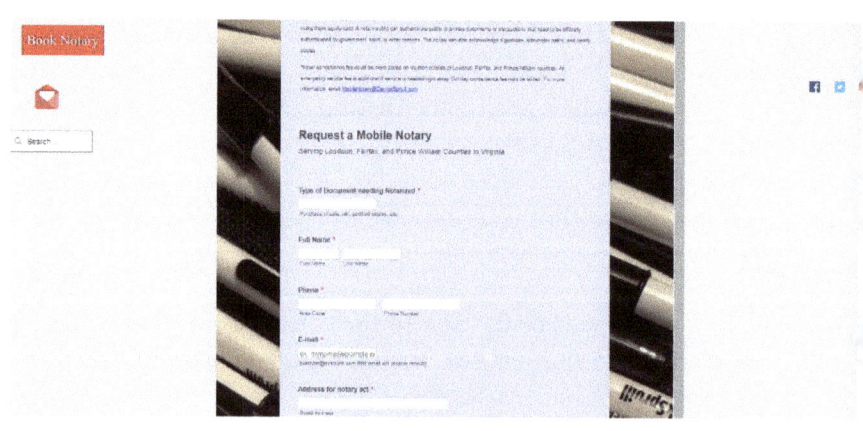

Courtesy of MobileNotarybyDerrickSpruill.com

LIST OF SERVICE OFFERINGS
Exercise 4.

1.

2.

3.

4.

5.

6.

7.

8.

9.

10.

Chapter 5

World Wide Web presence

In the beginning, there was the Internet. And the Internet indexes everything. And everything was found. Well, you get the point. I wanted my services to be found on the Internet. I had no intention of passing out flyers or going from location to location seeking customers at the wrong time. The power of the Internet could help customers find me when they need a service.

Once again, I researched all I could about search engine optimization (SEO), how people use the Internet, Web 3.0, how not to use search on the Internet, and so much more. I spent a lot of time building the website with SEO in mind. I invested time in learning about Google My Business for local searches. And the final product is what you see today for our business. The website could be better, but it compares well to large familiar household name brand companies and others when we use the Lighthouse plug-in to measure the speed and performance of the websites.

When setting up Google My Business free website from Google for businesses to be found on maps locally, we started by only filling in the basics. As time when on, we looked at other local companies and needed to strengthen our SEO for our Business page.

On the Google My Business page, we set the following:

1. Address
2. The hours of operation
3. Data collection form to make an appointment line.
4. Our website pages.
5. List of our Services
6. The area we service.

7. Prices
8. Pictures
9. Description of who we are.
10. Logo

This was only some of what we could add to the Google My Business page. Other attributes can be added. You will see our business on an Internet search in the picture below. The search engine lists this business in this fashion, making the company stand out in the search results. Getting found on the internet takes time and patience. At the beginning of the search for Mobile Notary by Derrick Spruill, we had only one paragraph, as you would see at the bottom of the picture. As time went on and more pages were indexed, a more professional look evolved.

Every day I look up my business on the internet. Every day I look at my competition on the Internet. I was analyzing what I was missing and what they were adding. I picked the top three mobile notaries that surfaced at the top of maps when searched locally and focused on ensuring I had more information available than they did. In the beginning, this was hard. This was the first time I built a website outside my college assignments. I did not have any content to add. The process was long.

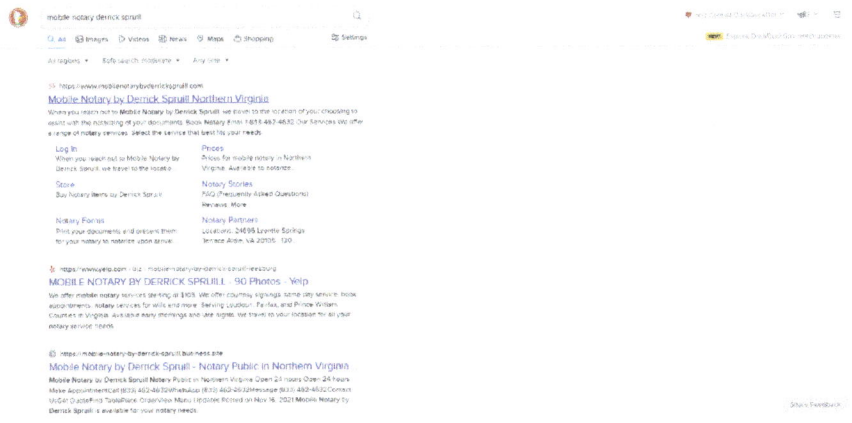

Visit MobileNotarybyDerrickSpruill.com

I came across this term called backlinks. Back to my main webpage, I discovered that backlinks are links from other websites. This was one of many tools that would help me rank the page. I started adding social media pages that connected to Mobile Notary by Derrick Spruill's website. I connected the Square processing websites and other platforms to the websites, allowing the web crawlers to build a web of connections to Mobile Notary by Derrick Spruill.

Later we begin to seek out reviews from customers. These reviews were a huge push for our business. Some of the challenges to getting reviews came from customers needing more time, customers needing to learn how to navigate to reviews on Google and reviews on Facebook or Yelp, or customers needing help to use the computer at all, getting their service by calling us.

Today when using a chatbot to ask what a mobile notary by Derrick Spruill is, the picture highlights the response from information gathered from the internet. Fascinating. Other attributes that contribute to ranking on the Internet:

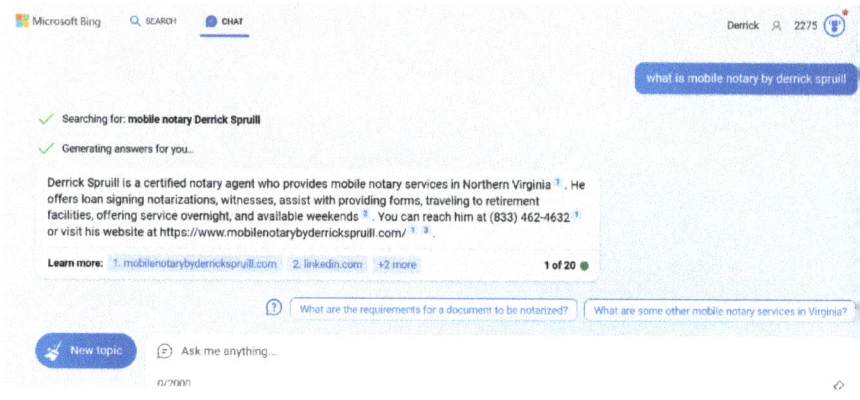

Visit MobileNotarybyDerrickSpruill.com

Target pages with reasonable keywords
Learn how every word and picture affects SEO on a webpage.
Make explicit statements on the webpage.
Add meaningful visuals.
Learn about meta tags.
Mine your search queries.
Add how-to videos.
Research SERP analysis

All on this list is extra. First, you want to be a mobile notary, so return to these advanced tips when you have time.

MAKE A CHECKLIST TO IMPROVE WEBSITE RANKING.

Exercise 5.

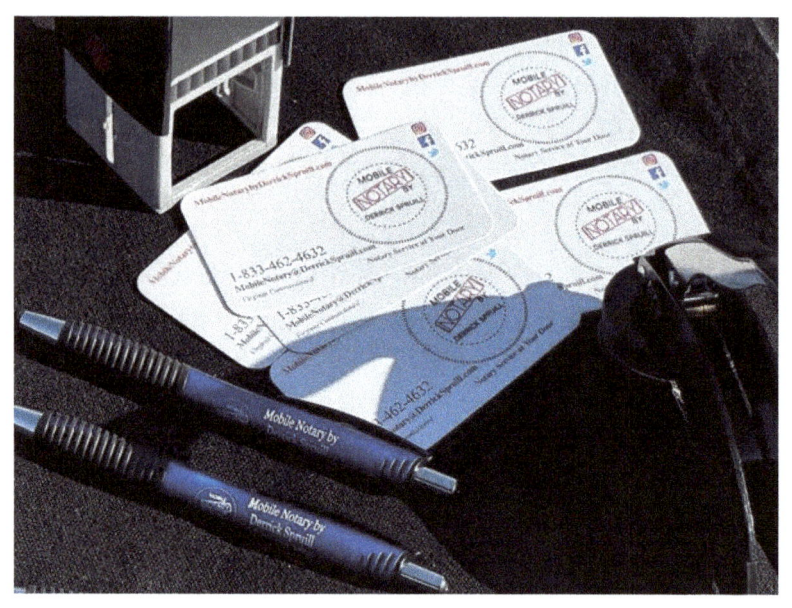

Illustration and photo by Montes Travis

Chapter 6

Who is my competition, and what are they doing?

Our research began with searching the internet for mobile notaries in our local area. We sought out whom to model and who would be our competition. Our business plan involved being the best unique mobile notary offering all the services possible to our county. Our goals:

1. Outperform our competitor on Internet search organically.
2. Be visible on maps when searching for keywords.
3. Establish a professional and trustworthy presence.
4. Provide services the competition does not offer.

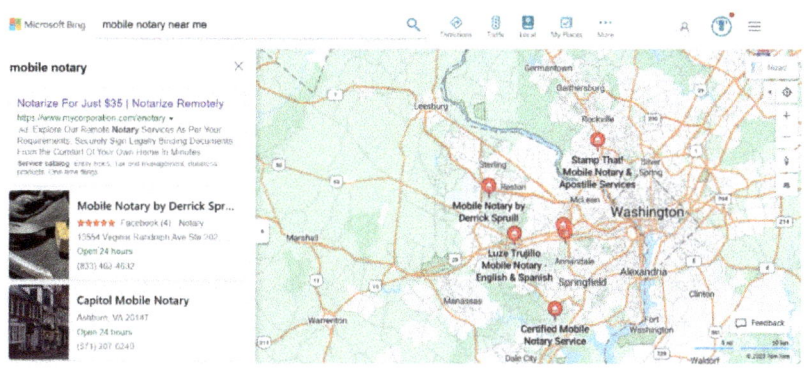

Visit MobileNotarybyDerrickSpruill.com

We started with completing our Google My Business profile. We added a list of services, and we added all the prices for each service. In the beginning, many of our competitors did not add fees online, and we thought this would be the main point of difference that would set us apart, straightforward, simple pricing. We decided on the service area and distance we wanted to travel. We connected the Google My Business page to our professional website. We set up the chat feature and connected our business telephone number. Later we started taking lots of pictures for our website and business. These pictures would be used for Twitter, Facebook, Instagram, and Google My Business page updates. We wanted to build something other mobile notaries did not have with these pictures, still shots of notary stamps and supplies. We took hundreds of images, which became a unique branding with Mobile Notary by Derrick Spruill. No other notary business in the area presented multiple images on their website, and one of our goals was accomplished *(Provide what the competition does not)*.

We added a social news account with updates adding trustworthiness to the Internet algorithm. We added a social media account for posting our pictures, and later we developed a friend's connection social account for Mobile Notary by Derrick Spruill. Our most significant point of difference was adding an online data collection form webpage to our website and Google My Business page.

The online data collection form allowed customers to book an appointment by date and time. The form allowed them to add their address of service with their information. The form allowed them to pick the service they wanted with all the add-on services. And finally, the JotForm allowed the customer to pay for mobile notary services in advance. This was huge for us; no local mobile notary offered this feature. We soon had customers who would book appointments in the middle of the night for a service date seven days in advance. This lets us know we found our customer and the price was right. We later discussed our findings; for a person to search the internet, complete their research, and trust entering their credit card information online in the middle of the night, let us know we accomplished one of our goals *(Look professional and trustworthy)*.

We sought to be a strong brand like the larger national and international businesses worldwide. We had title companies booking appointments. We had lawyers and their paralegals booking appointments. We even had customers from Europe and Asia book appointments online for their CEOs living or visiting the area.

This online data collection form was new to this industry in this area. We found our niche market. We continued to share the link for customers to book appointments, letting them know this was a secure and easy way to pay for the mobile notary service before the notary appointment. We shared the link on our daily online updates; we shared the link on all our social platforms. We had other websites that offered their payment systems, but we opted to use our form instead for collecting appointments and payments.

It took less than one year for the Internet web crawlers to have our Google My Business webpage surface at the top of the search in the counties we serve. We invested much time into SEO and learned so much from the work. We did not invest money in advertising our website to customers. We allowed the web to do its job in due time. Today our website surfaces organically in most online searches.

We continue to watch our competition and see what new add-ons, features, or services they offer. We continue to ask customers for reviews to help with our ranking on the Internet. We continue to work with other search engines and review the search results for improvements. These search engines are our focus areas for improving our SEO organically with a search online. We continue examining what other mobile notaries do nationwide through website searches. We continue to review our local competition social media pages. We still looked for prices online, and one day we found someone that modeled our services and website. We were honored. After discovering this new competitor, we decided to continue our work to stay in first position with mobile notary service in our area. Most customers looking for a mobile notary would not look on page five for a service provider, but as a company, we do look on page five to see who our up-and-coming competition is. Relentlessly searching the Internet every week helps us monitor our competitors. It also allows us to review our information online and repair any broken links, misspellings, and insufficient information imputed wrong from third-party platforms.

COMPETITION IN AREA
Exercise 6.

1.

2.

3.

4.

5.

COMPETITION SERVICE OFFERINGS

1.

2.

3.

4.

5.

41

Illustration and photo by Montes Travis

Chapter 7

All about the Convenience

The environment in Northern Virginia is fast-paced. Traffic is always heavy, and people rush from point A to point B all day. With Washington, D.C., just next door across state lines, there is so much support for the government and the endless number of jobs servicing the United States and all its agencies. We have a hockey team here. We have a football team here, a basketball team, and other sporting groups. We also have two major airports less than 30 miles apart. This is an ideal place to set up shop as a mobile notary. There are Living Wills that need to be notarized. There are mortgage documents that need to be notarized. There are dignitaries from around the world that live in the area. They may have declarations to notaries, remote purchases that need to be notarized, and business deals that need to be implemented with a seal. This is where the convenience of having a mobile notary comes in to help customers.

We offer notaries services by traveling to the client's location with the charge of a traveling convenience fee. This fee is modest compared to the time it would take the client to travel to a bank or postal store. In Northern Virginia, time is money. Our clients are busy living, running their businesses, or traveling. We offer the convenience of traveling to the client just like food delivery brings customers food. We offer the convenience of traveling to the client, like same-day postal service delivery packages within two hours. The business model fits this area. Customers need this service from what we gathered from our feedback. This is part of our mobile notary work in Loudoun and Fairfax County. We also assist title companies, travel to retirement centers, and offer to retrieve documents from the courthouse. Convenience is our service. Convenience is what we offer, and convenience is who we are to the public.

WHAT WOULD YOU DESCRIBE AS CONVENIENCE?

Exercise 7.

Chapter 8

A Day as a mobile notary

The Hospital Visit: Notary Stories by Derrick Spruill

Illustration by Montes Travis

Today, I assisted a client at a local hospital during a rainy night. I received a phone call from a woman, and we made an appointment to meet. As I prepared to travel, I received a second phone call from a doctor from the exact location, telling me to hurry because the client was undergoing surgery. I arrived earlier than expected after a short drive in the foggy weather.

Once I arrived at the hospital to meet the client, I noticed he was experiencing much pain from a recent car accident. I was in a daze or cloud from all the commotion in the hallways

47

and room. The client was able to talk. He was even making jokes. His girlfriend and his assistant joined him. It was 2:00 a.m., and he needed papers notarized to release his vehicle from the impound.

I will always remember the words he said to me. He said, "Never drive when in rage; driving requires too much focus. Don't get caught up in a conversation over the phone and forget where you are. Let everyone know- to stay in the moment." Today's takeaway is to stay in the moment and focus on one thing at a time giving your undivided attention to that person or task, but not both.

At the Hotel: Notary Stories by Derrick Spruill

Illustration by Montes Travis

It's now 4:15 p.m. I've been waiting in the fancy hotel lobby since 4:00 p.m. A client had already prepaid for me to notarize a new vehicle purchase. As I look across the hall, I see a couple coming from the ballroom. The bride is wearing a beautiful yellow dress with a 12 ft. train. The groom is wearing the most stylish blue tuxedo I have ever seen, with a fabulous top hat to match.

They're walking in my direction. The room is erupting with people from all directions. I was amazed that they were looking at me. To my surprise, my clients had just gotten married. The

49

bride was purchasing a new luxury vehicle, and I was asked to notarize the paperwork after her wedding before the reception. Wow, talk about structured timing. In a tiny chit-chat, I congratulated the bride on her marriage and purchasing her new vehicle. She was pleased and ecstatic, and she was crying in disbelief. Her honeymoon was abroad, and she was leaving tonight.

I was in disbelief, too, at this moment, witnessing everything happening. After she finished signing all the documents her assistant provided, she asked me to join the family in the reception area. I had to decline respectfully. I had another scheduled appointment. I realize people can do whatever they want; plan for it.

The Little Piece of Heaven: Notary Stories by Derrick Spruill

Illustration by Montes Travis

After driving for 45 minutes into the Appalachian Mountains, I found myself traveling down a dirt gravel road. The scenery was beautiful. The weather was terrific. I even rolled down my window to take in the moment of the fresh air. As I looked to the right, I could see the rolling hills of nothing but green grass and trees. As I looked to the left, I saw beautiful million-dollar homes nestled in between tall oaks and pine trees. I continued to drive for another couple of miles before coming across this house, which looked to have been built in the 1800s.

I was sitting on a piece of land between new modern-day mansions refusing to be removed or bulldozed from existence. I came across this piece of heaven that has been undisturbed by all the construction around it from the last century. This home was a paradise where my client had been living all his life. He had booked and prepaid for a notary online. He made an appointment a week in advance, and I was able to meet him today. I was amazed at what I would find in the middle of nowhere or the middle of heaven.

When I left the client's home and I started driving away, it took my breath away to have walked into a building, a small house with two bedrooms, still standing after 120 years. I realized how much has changed over the last one hundred years and how much things are made the same, like tables, chairs, doors, paintings and picture frames, photographs, window seals, fireplaces, shingles on buildings, air conditioner in the window, and the many carpets throughout the home. I had to appreciate the long life of people, the durability of goods, longevity, and peace on earth.

What would it be like to live in such a place for so long, so far from my hustle and bustle world, surrounded by people from every walk of life, stuck in traffic, rushing from here to there all day? I was touched by that moment by what true peace of mind felt like on this day. It was bliss.

Illustration and photo by Montes Travis

Chapter 9

37 Professional Tips for
MOBILE NOTARIES

1. **Always dress professionally.** Ensure your clothes are ironed, your shoes are clean, and your hair is presentable. When you meet with a client, they are looking for someone professional they can trust with their documents, which could be valued at $1,500,000 for a home, $200,000 for an automobile, or even $36 million for a will or trust. So, look the part by looking professional.

2. **Always be on time. Arrive before the scheduled time.** The client's time is expected to be precious for the charged price. When clients take the time to go online, book an appointment, and prepay for a service without talking to anyone, they expect what they pay for without excuse. Excuses only satisfy the individual providing the excuse.

3. **Be prepared before traveling to the client.** Research what the client may need before your arrival. When in doubt, bring an extra form just in case the client needs to correct the form or makes a mistake on the form. We have an attachment tab on our online data collection form for clients to attach for review before we arrive. This is another option for the client to use. We bring two copies of a form just in case the client needs these forms. Our website has free forms for clients to download, print, and present to the notary when we arrive. Several clients have printed these free forms and have them ready for the notary to notarize their signatures on arrival. We provide affiliate form services on our website as well.

4. **Carry plenty of ink pens to the signing.** Bring at least two black ink pens and at least two blue ink pens. Some documents from different states may require a particular pen color. The client may also have specific requests as well. And if an ink pen stops working, you have a spare one. There's nothing more professional than having a backup plan and accommodating the client when the needs arise.

5. **Carry more than one notary stamp to the signing.** We carry small circle notary stamps. We carry rectangular self-inking stamps. We also carry embosser stamps if the client wants a little extra touch. The document may not have enough space for the regularly used stamp. We provide gold circle stickers as a little extra when using our embosser seal. We also use our ink stamps for replication and for filing scanned documents.

6. **Use Online Forms to collect information and payment.** We use an online data collection form for clients to request and book a notary. Our clients can select from a list of the many services we offer, add their personal information, select the date and time for the appointment, attach a document for use to review, and provide payment if they choose to. This form also provides details for emailing us, an explanation of cost and services, service areas, and cancelation charges. They can pay by credit card, Apple Pay, Cash App, or Google Pay.

7. **Maximize all the features of Google My Business Page**. Make sure to fill out every part of the My Business Page, from the address, the services, the website link, pictures, updates, offers, prices, holiday hours, and more. Adding all this information builds creditability for your website connection on the Internet. It may not happen all in one sitting, so continue to add new information over time. Internet crawlers love to find new information.

8. **Get a professional email address.** We started using our email address from day one by adding MobileNotary@DerrickSpruill.com to our toolbox. It looks professional and easy to associate with the business name. This does come with a monthly cost. It makes for great branding. It looks great with the business name on the business card to help clients remember the name of the business when searching Mobile Notary by Derrick Spruill or when visiting MobileNotarybyDerrickSpruill.com.

9. **Add a professional email signature.** We use free software to add a professional email address for our business. Our signature has our logo, phone number, website, main company address, social links, a button for clients to book a notary, a confidential communication declaimer, and a link to leave a review online.

10. **Connect your Online Forms to your calendar.** When a client books a notary online, we have our

calendar synced so this information is fed into our calendar immediately. This helps us by not missing any appointments or serves as a reminder every day until the appointment time.

11. **Buy a dual scanner printer for printing services.** Once you get established, buy a fast scanner printer that will help with scanning load documents for clients. Buy one that can load legal-size and letter-size paper. Outside of working for large notary mortgage signing service companies, we scan copies and email our clients so they can always have a soft digital copy in their email. Having a notarized scanned copy in an email will prove valuable when needed if it is not filed with the clerk of court. Also, having a printer allows you to offer the service of printing documents for an individual who may not have a printer. They can email the documents to you, print them, and bring them to the signing for a fee.

12. **Make available multiple payment options.** We accept cash and checks from all our clients. Our bank checks are mobile deposited into our business checking accounts moments after the signing. We send a receipt by email once the bank checks are deposited. We accept credit and debit card payments through our primary processing services. We also offer payments by PayPal, Cash App, Zelle, and KoronaPay (for overseas transactions). These payment processors allow us to send an invoice, request payment, and sell our services online. Please refrain from making it painful for a client to pay. No large business poses this issue when collecting payment from their clients. This pain point does not exist. Always keep your systems up to date and

ready for use. You may or may not use them, but you may have one customer who wants to pay a certain way, giving you a professional look.

13. **Set your prices in advance for your clients.** We set our prices online. Every service has a fixed price. We offer traveling notary services. We offer loan signing agents. We offer an apostille service. We provide services for printed documents. We set our price for i9 employment verification. We have prices for fingerprinting. We have a fixed price for Concierge Service and fees designated for document delivery services with the major delivery carriers. The professional look is the same as large restaurant chains. They have a menu board. The price is set and simple. This will provide confidence for each of your clients and possibly repeat business.

14. **Take business cards to every signing.** Have some professionally made business cards to provide to each of your clients upon arriving at the signing. Supply a business card to everyone at the signing, like when witnesses are present. This added touch adds creditability when you arrive, putting the client at ease.

15. **Set up an account with the leading package delivery carriers.** These companies may offer discount pricing to businesses when printing labels for shipping from your computer with your business account. It is convenient for you, so you can drop the package off at the counter, saving time. If you offer this service, you can have the label set up and printed before arriving at the signing. How awesome is it for a client to seek out

to have a document notarized by you and delivered to the local package delivery store all in one service? Professional and above expectations. With these accounts, you can provide the tracking numbers to the clients for easy tracking as an extra touch of service.

16. **Carry printed forms to every signing.** We have come across some of the same everyday events from time to time. We bring consent forms, a Department of Motor Vehicles Bill of Sale form, and a notary acknowledgment form, to name a few. Having these forms available have been life savers on time. We conduct much business at the airport. So, when a customer needs help because they did not think they needed such a form, we are Johnny-on-the-spot with the papers providing that extra professional service they may have yet to expect. Did I say it saves time having to go and print the document off?

17. **Having a portable tablet and hotspot available for i9 verification.** We offer this service. We have completed a paper copy of employment verification. We have completed emailed verification, and we have had to log onto a website for a company with authorization to verify the client's identity.

18. **Showing empathy, sympathy, or emotions when required.** Some situations may require this. Compassion may be needed when traveling to a hospital for an injured person who needs a release form for an impounded automobile notarized. The correct emotional response may be required when sitting with a doctor and a patient behind closed doors. Sympathy

may be needed during a signing event with lawyers and clients reviewing probate documents. Possess the correct emotional IQ for each type of situation so you will be a correct lasting response to the moment.

19. **Build a professional website.** We built our website and spent hundreds of hours improving our SEO over the years. We use the Lighthouse plugin to measure our success compared to other websites. We are proud of our success. We have had better results than large banks, nationwide restaurant chains, and hotel websites when using the Lighthouse free plugin to measure results from any website you may search. Our website is not just an information page; it collects payment, provides notary news, offers free forms for clients to download and use, the website answers many frequently asked questions, and shares reviews from past clients. Clients worldwide can look us up, email us from our website, learn about the services we offer, take note of the prices we charge, and make a one-time payment if needed. Our Search Engine Optimization has helped us conduct business with clients from Greece, Korea, and Spain. Clients from Florida, New York, California, Texas, Arizona, and Michigan. These clients see our website as official; they see it as trustworthy, and they are confident that we can provide the services they may request of us.

20. **Sync your documents to the cloud.** When you need to print a form or have a copy emailed to a client, the only place you have it is on your computer; if it were in the cloud, you would be able to pull this document at any time you are away from the computer at ease directly from your phone. This system saves time when the client needs information immediately when you're

not at your computer. Say you need a w-9 form sent to a new firm you work for. If you have one saved on your company and your cloud is linked to your phone, it will save you so much time and make you look like a superstar being able to send that form to the client within minutes of the request.

21. **Carry clipboards to signings**. We bring clipboards with us for every signing. This helps with ensuring the document signature is captured correctly. Having a ridged wood grain surface could cause problems when signing multiple documents. We bring clipboards to assist when an older adult in bed may need a flat surface to sign on.

22. **Get a true-copy stamp.** This has helped us look more professional when providing a true copy as a notarial act. We may need to ensure that a copy of a college degree is a true copy. A true-copy stamp that looks professional and readily available will impress the client with your experience.

23. **Get a Jurat Stamp.** This stamp has helped us tremendously. This stamp includes all the correct verbiage, saving time for writing these exact words for the client. These stamps can come available with the notary's name and number or without it, as the notary would fill in this information and sign.

24. **Use a pluck form case to carry notary supplies.** We have tailored man notary cases with a space for each of our notary tools. As we unpack for the signing,

everything is easy to find and stays put. When we pack up to leave, we can quickly identify any items left behind before leaving the signing. We carry notary two stamps, fingerprinting stamps, an embosser, gold seal stickers, blue and black ink pens, two clipboards, a true-copy stamp, a jurat stamp, a credit card reader, wipes, spare paper, and blank notary forms. We started this setup after three years. We wanted to add that professional look when we arrived at the signings.

25. **Be present with the client.** Contrary to what others may suggest, we believe what customers are for us will be for us, and what customers we miss are not for us. We silence our phones for the few minutes we spend with each client. Our client pays for this moment. It may only be about 15 to 30 minutes, but this is their time alone. If our phone vibrates on our hip, we do not answer at that moment. It may not be for us if a customer does not leave a message. It would be the same if we were in the restroom washing our hands and unable to answer the phone—one quality moment per customer at a time.

26. **Review your worldwide presence regularly.** We often review our websites for broken links and search our business name to see what is online about our business. We perform a search and see what comes up. We edit where possible and correct any changes. We also check all the links from and to our websites. Sometimes they need to be fixed, which could lead to lost customers. So, review often for assurance.

27. **Review your competition regularly.** We check the internet to see where we stand with our competition. We need to see if our competitors are leapfrogging us with SEO, adapting their services, or improving their websites with additional features. We want to continue to grow our business and look for other ways to reach new customers. We want to benchmark where we stand with our direct competition and ensure we provide what our clients look for in a mobile notary.

28. **Ask customers for reviews.** This one has helped us to skyrocket to the top of the webpage search as credibility from Google. Google looks to us as an authority figure when it comes to mobile notary services in the areas we serve. This took time. As customers started to share their feedback on our services, Google decided it was important for others looking for our services to know.

29. **Have the postal service carriers' regular envelopes available.** We keep one or two of each readily available for every visit. We can provide this additional service when a client wants the notarized document mailed immediately after the signing appointment. We would drop the envelope off as requested and send them a picture for reassurance of completion. Another service to offer and impress the client when they least expect.

30. **Bring a desk flip calendar to a signing appointment.** When traveling to a living will or estate signing and having multiple signers and witnesses, we bring a bright red and white flip calendar to our signing for our client to reference during the signing. It is always amazing to see everyone repeatedly ask, "What is

today's date" during the signing. So, by bringing a sizeable five-by-six-inch flip calendar to the signing, everyone can look up from time to time to see the date as needed when having to sign multiple pages needing dates. This extra peace of mind puts everyone at ease, not having to open their phone or look around. This adds a professional look.

31. **Use social media to promote your web presence.** As I mentioned, promoting your business on social media can lead customers to your website page, producing backlinks for Internet crawlers to search. We only use a few primary social media platforms. Today there could be over 30 different platforms to socialize with others who think like you. This is a great way to let the world know your business exists.

32. **Sign up for Notary Service Contract Companies.** We initially signed up and started working for twelve large companies. We learned so much from these companies allowing us only to use them when we want to. In the beginning, we labeled these companies as paid training. We made mistakes, and we had to go back to the customer. We didn't set the printer settings correctly before scanning or getting the documents dropped timely. Like an amateur, our dollar per hour was meager. After our first 90 days of learning so much from one another and seeing so many different documents, we have become professionals today and offer many other services.

33. **Use video-making solutions for marketing purposes.** We came across these video makers and wanted to explore simple, easy-to-use methods to deliver our message. We are open for business as mobile notaries. Since adding these videos to our site and the updates to social media links and Google My Business page, we see these videos surface at the top of the rankings for our business. These easy-to-use video-making software are must-haves. They are nice to have, especially with the add-on features.

34. **Use YouTube.** We added a few videos of Mobile Notary by Derrick Spruill to YouTube. These videos added a little touch to our business that helped us stand out from our competition. Making these videos allowed us to continue to love and enjoy the company we work in while taking a break and enjoying our successes.

35. **Provide additional witnesses.** If you can, set this up to work for your area. So many families are being relocated to this area, and they have yet to have time to involve neighbors in their busy lives. Bringing a witness to the signing event is more than a great service offering. Some customers have called the service a blessing and convenient. Mobile Notary by Derrick Spruill has over four contacts available at different times when an additional witness is needed at a signing. These friends of the business are paid the full flat witness fee for their 30 minutes. This service provides peace of mind for the client when time is more critical.

36. **Conduct research and never stop learning.** Just like you are doing today, looking for more information. For each signing, we travel to assist; different clients have different types of forms for other events. We have come across last wills and testaments in various states requiring different tasks to be executed and locations to notarize. The same is true for all the other loan documents from all fifty states. We say yes to every job that needs to be completed by a mobile notary. When encountering something new, we research how to execute the signing event properly. We also continue to study and learn about the changing notary laws.

37. **Have Fun.** Enjoy what you do every day. Every time we travel to assist a client, we learn more about the world. We make new friends and acquaintances every time we travel to a client. We enjoy serving others, and we find it very rewarding to serve the community of Northern Virginia. Find your joy in helping others and be open to assisting clients from all different walks of life.

Illustration and photo by Montes Travis

Chapter 10
Scheduling Appointments

Scheduling each notary appointment at the appropriate time is critical to our successful notary business. We have succeeded in making the schedule paramount, ensuring customer service time is allotted by not overbooking our clients. We have also made scheduling a priority to not cause any conflict with other obligations in our family lives. We are constantly managing our schedules meticulously. This means we put every appointment on our calendars. Each of us ensures every doctor's and dentist's appointment is added to their calendar with the location of the doctor's or dentist's address. All calendars are shared for complete visibility.

We do not schedule clients back-to-back, allowing extra time for mistakes or services the current client may want to add. Early in our notary business, we learned that upselling services might cause spare time for us to stay over at a client's location. Some of these additional services would be delivering a package to the postal store or scanning documents to have emailed to clients. Either way, we need to always account for these surprises.

Our clients can book appointments online through our website. These appointments are automatically fed into our calendars. We have alerts set when clients book appointments without talking to a notary. We follow up with an email after the autoresponder sends confirmation.

Our online data collection form easily captures the customer's name, address, service request, time, and payment. The information gathered is so convenient for mapping addresses, tracking customer information for journaling, and milage tracking fed into other apps. The online forms have saved us so much time.

For every appointment, we aim to arrive at least five minutes early. These few extra minutes allow for time to find parking, prepare to meet with the client or gather us after so much driving throughout the day. Our schedule also allows for undevoted time with the client, like staying in the moment and not worrying about getting to the next appointment. This part of the schedule helps us to be more human and show we care when engaging the client.

We have had clients cancel their appointments. We have had extra time to show up unplanned after these cancelations. All our scheduled appointments have been paid for in advance, so in extreme circumstances, we point our customers to the canceled appointments policy we have added to our payment forms.

If you are not using a calendar for your mobile notary services, we encourage you to. These have been very beneficial to use.

WHAT WOULD YOU PUT ON YOUR SCHEDULE?
Exercise 8.

Where does this QRC take you?

Photo by Montes Travis

ABOUT THE AUTHOR

DERRICK SPRUILL

Derrick lives in Herndon, Virginia, and works as a district support store manager for a large pharmacy chain. He's associated with World Changers Ministries. He loves NASCAR and NFL Football. He is a Dale Earnhardt, Joey Logano, and Kyle Busch fan and has been a Cincinnati Bengals fan since the days of the Icky Woods shuffle. He spends his free time reading all things business. He has an MBA in Human Resources and a bachelor's in accounting from Walden University. After working for over 25 years for Fortune 100 businesses, Derrick and his partners decided to start their business ventures for themselves—Derrick fathers four adult children, Derrick Jr, Jessica Liann, Fran-Kee Nicole, and Frank Darren.

Contact the author via Derrick@DerrickSpruill.com to inform us of any needed book corrections or typos. Share your ideas with us so we can share those ideas with others.

Call 1-833-462-4632 for more information.
Visit MobileNotarybyDerrickSpruill.com to get more ideas.

Follow us on Facebook!
https://www.facebook.com/MobileNotarybyDerrick

Follow us on Twitter!
https://twitter.com/byNotary

Follow us on Instagram!
https://www.instagram.com/mobilenotaryby/

We offer 1-on-1 coaching services. We provide speaking engagements. We offer other services, i.e., steps to starting a business and efforts to hire a team.

Mobile Notary by Derrick Spruill is serving the public one notary act at a time.

Published by Magnificent Workz Business Solutions

www.ingramcontent.com/pod-product-compliance
Lightning Source LLC
Chambersburg PA
CBHW051230120626
46547CB00013B/1591